THE CANADIAN BRASS
15 FAVORITE HYMNS
EASY ARRANGEMENTS

ARRANGED BY LARRY MOORE

T0059262

2   All Creatures of Our God and King

4   All Glory, Laud, and Honor

6   Blessed Assurance

8   Christ the Lord Is Risen Today

10   Come, Ye Thankful People, Come

12   Crown Him With Many Crowns

14   Fairest Lord Jesus

16   For the Beauty of the Earth

18   God of Our Fathers

20   Guide Me, O Thou Great Jehovah

22   Holy, Holy, Holy!

24   Joyful, Joyful, We Adore Thee

26   Lead On, O King Eternal

28   A Mighty Fortress Is Our God

30   O God, Our Help in Ages Past

Using the Arrangements

A music director/conductor can come up with various approaches to a hymn. For instance: verse 1 – no brass; verse 2 – brass (Standard Version); verse 3 – brass (Variation Verse); verse 4 – brass (Standard Version) with Trumpet Descant. Or, another example might be: verse 1 – brass (Standard Version) with keyboard; verse 2 – brass (Standard Version), no keyboard; verse 3 – brass (Variation Verse). Get creative!

Optional Trumpet Descant

The Conductor's Score also includes the part for a trumpet descant. The descant may be added to any of the Standard Version verses of a hymn. The trumpet part is available in the following Hal Leonard publication: 50485217 *The Canadian Brass: 15 Favorite Hymns–Trumpet Descants*

Visit the official website of The Canadian Brass:
www.canbrass.com

HAL•LEONARD®
CORPORATION

7777 W. BLUEMOUND RD. P.O. BOX 13819 MILWAUKEE, WI 53213

Visit Hal Leonard Online at
www.halleonard.com

Keyboard
(optional)

CANADIAN BRASS

ALL CREATURES OF OUR GOD AND KING

LASST UNS ERFREUEN

Francis of Assisi
Trans. W.H. Draper

Geistliche Kirchengesang
Harmonized by Ralph Vaughan Williams

STANDARD VERSION
Joyously (♩ = 120)

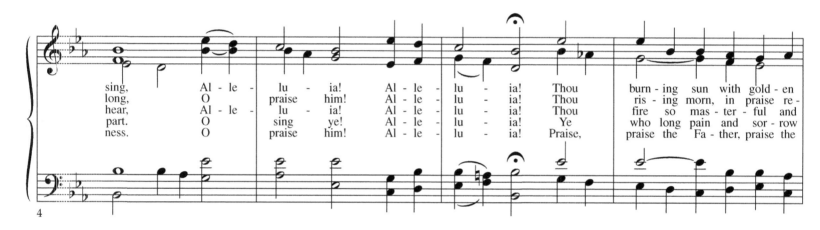

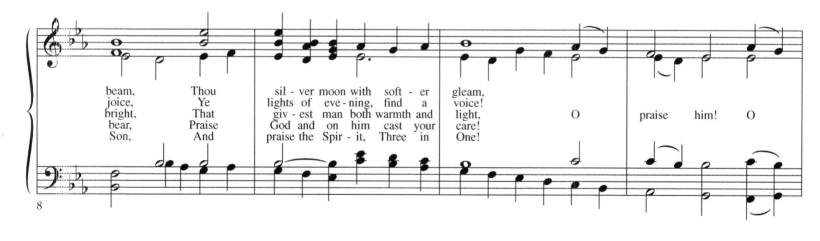

Repeat as needed (opt.)   Amen   VARIATION VERSE

ia!   A - men.   ia!

* *rit.* is used only if the Variation Verse is played as the final verse

Return to Standard Version as needed

Keyboard
(optional)

CANADIAN BRASS
ALL GLORY, LAUD, AND HONOR
ST. THEODULPH

Theodulph of Orleans, ca. 820
Trans. by John Mason Neal, 1851; alt., 1859

Melchior Teschner, 1615

STANDARD VERSION

Regally (♩ = 108)

1. All glory, laud, and hon - or To thee, Re - deem - er, King,
2. Thou art the King of Is - rael, Thou Da - vid's roy - al son,
3. Thou did'st ac - cept their prais - es; Ac - cept the prayers we bring,

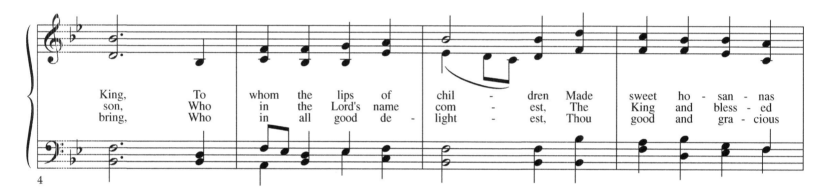

To whom the lips of chil - dren Made sweet ho - san - nas ring!
Who in the Lord's name com - est, The King and bless - ed One;
Who in all good de - light - est, Thou good and gra - cious King.

The peo - ple of the He - brews With palms be - fore thee went;
To thee, be - fore thy pas - sion, They sang their hymns of praise;
All glo - ry, laud, and hon - or To thee, Re - deem - er, King,

Our praise and prayer and an - thems Be - fore thee we pre -
To thee, now high ex - alt - ed, Our mel - o - dy we
To whom the lips of chil - dren Made sweet ho - san - nas

Repeat as needed (opt.)

sent.
raise.
ring!

Amen

A - men.

VARIATION VERSE

sent.
raise.
ring!

16

20

24

(rit.)*

28

32

* *rit.* is used only if the Variation Verse is played as the final verse

Return to Standard Version as needed

Keyboard
(optional)

CANADIAN BRASS
BLESSED ASSURANCE
ASSURANCE

Fanny J. Crosby

Phoebe P. Knapp

STANDARD VERSION
Spirited (♩. = 80)

1. Bless-ed as - sur - ance, Je - sus is mine! O what a fore - taste of glo - ry di -
2. Per - fect sub - mis - sion, per - fect de - light! Vi - sions of rap - ture now burst on my
3. Per - fect sub - mi - sion, all is at rest, I in my Sav - ior am hap - py and

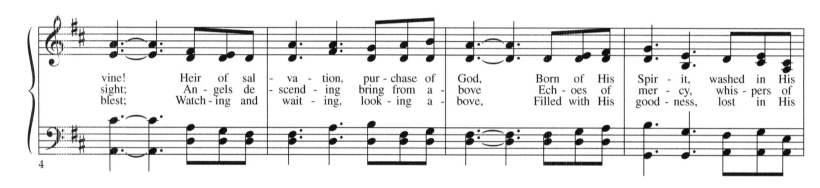

vine! Heir of sal - va - tion, pur - chase of God, Born of His Spir - it, washed in His
sight; An - gels de - scend - ing bring from a - bove Ech - oes of mer - cy, whis - pers of
blest; Watch - ing and wait - ing, look - ing a - bove, Filled with His good - ness, lost in His

blood.
love. This is my sto - ry, this is my song, Prais - ing my Sav - ior all the day
love.

long; This is my sto - ry, this is my song, Prais - ing my Sav - ior all the day

Repeat as needed (opt.) | VARIATION VERSE

long.

long.

16

19

22

26

30

rit. is used only if the Variation Verse is played as the final verse

Return to Standard Version as needed

CANADIAN BRASS

CHRIST THE LORD IS RISEN TODAY

EASTER HYMN

Charles Wesley

from *Lyra Davidica*, London, 1708

STANDARD VERSION
Joyously (♩ = 120)

1. Christ the Lord is ris'n to - day,		Al - le - lu - ia!
2. Lives a - gain our glo - rious King,		Al - le - lu - ia!
3. Love's re - deem - ing work is done,		Al - le - lu - ia!
4. Soar we now where Christ has led,		Al - le - lu - ia!

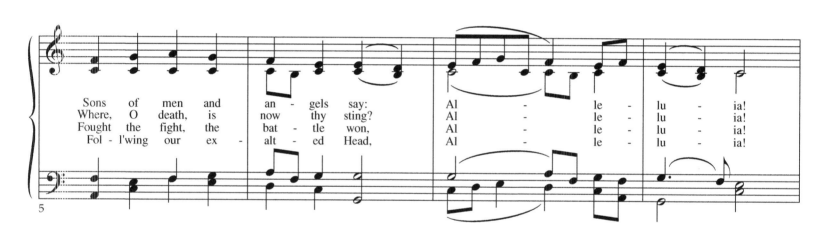

Sons of men and an - gels say:		Al - le - lu - ia!
Where, O death, is now thy sting?		Al - le - lu - ia!
Fought the fight, the bat - tle won,		Al - le - lu - ia!
Fol - l'wing our ex - alt - ed Head,		Al - le - lu - ia!

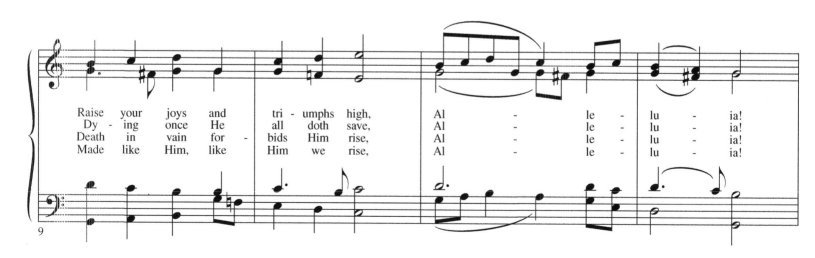

Raise your joys and tri - umphs high,		Al - le - lu - ia!
Dy - ing once He all doth save,		Al - le - lu - ia!
Death in vain for - bids Him rise,		Al - le - lu - ia!
Made like Him, like Him we rise,		Al - le - lu - ia!

Repeat as needed (opt.)

Sing, ye heav'ns, and earth re - ply: Al - le - lu - ia!
Where thy vic - to - ry, O grave? Al - le - lu - ia!
Christ has o - pened Par - a - dise, Al - le - lu - ia!
Ours the cross, the grave, the skies, Al - le - lu - ia!

VARIATION VERSE

(rit.)*

* *rit.* is used only if the Variation Verse is played as the final verse

Return to Standard Version as needed

Keyboard
(optional)

CANADIAN BRASS

COME, YE THANKFUL PEOPLE, COME

ST. GEORGE'S, WINDSOR

Henry Alford

George J. Elvey

STANDARD VERSION

Regally (♩ = 120)

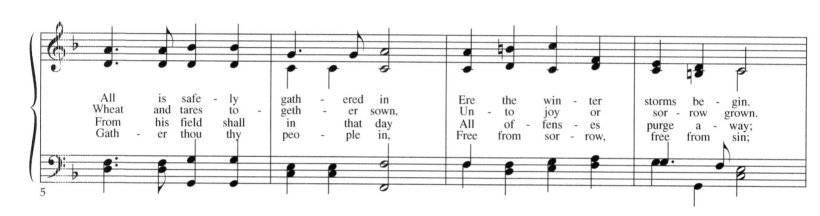

1. Come, ye thank-ful peo - ple, come Raise the song of har - vest home:
2. All the world is God's own field, Fruit un - to his praise to yield;
3. For the Lord our God shall come And shall take his har - vest home;
4. E - ven so, Lord, quick - ly come To Thy fi - nal har - vest home;

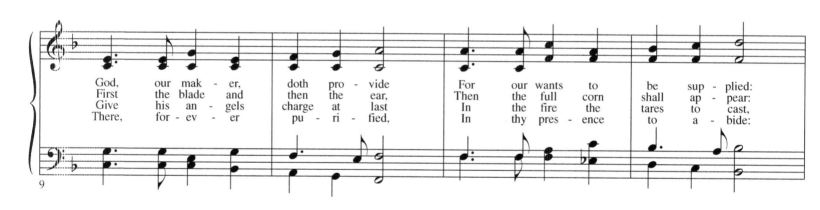

All is safe - ly gath - ered in, Ere the win - ter storms be - gin.
Wheat and tares to - geth - er sown, Un - to joy or sor - row grown.
From his field shall in that day All of - fens - es purge a - way;
Gath - er thou thy peo - ple in, Free from sor - row, free from sin;

God, our mak - er, doth pro - vide For our wants to be sup - plied:
First the blade and then the ear, Then the full corn shall ap - pear:
Give his an - gels charge at last In the fire the tares to cast,
There, for - ev - er pu - ri - fied, In thy pres - ence to a - bide:

Repeat as needed (opt.)

Come to God's own tem - ple, come, Raise the song of har - vest home.
First the blade and Whole - some grain and pure may be.
Lord of har - vest, grant that we In his gar - ner ev - er - more.
But the fruit - ful ears to store
Come, with all thine an - gels, come Raise the glo - rious har - vest home.

* *rit.* is used only if the Variation Verse is played as the final verse

Return to Standard Version as needed

CANADIAN BRASS
CROWN HIM WITH MANY CROWNS
DIADEMATA

Matthew Bridges, stanzas 1,2,4;
Godfrey Thring, stanza 3

George J. Elvey

STANDARD VERSION
Stately (♩ = 112)

1. Crown Him with man - y crowns, The Lamb up - on His throne: Hark!
2. Crown Him the Lord of love: Be - hold His hands and side: Rich
3. Crown Him the Lord of life: Who tri - umphed o'er the grave, Who
4. Crown Him the Lord of heav'n: One with the Fa - ther known, One

how the heav'n - ly an - them drowns All mu - sic but its own! A -
wounds, yet vis - i - ble a - bove, In beau - ty glo - ri - fied. No
rose vic - to - rious to the strife For those He came to save. His
with the Spir - it through Him giv'n From yon - der glo - rious throne. To

wake, my soul, and sing Of Him who died for thee, And
an - gel in the sky Can ful - ly bear that sight, But
glo - ries now we sing, Who died and rose on high, Who
Thee be end - less praise, For Thou for us hast died; Be

Repeat as needed (opt.)

hail Him as thy match - less King Through all e - ter - ni - ty.
down - ward bends his won - d'ring eye At mys - ter - ies so bright.
died e - ter - nal life to bring and lives that death may die.
Thou, O Lord, through end - less days A - dored and mag - ni - fied.

* *rit.* is used only if the Variation Verse is played as the final verse

Return to Standard Version as needed

CANADIAN BRASS

Keyboard
(optional)

FAIREST LORD JESUS
(Beautiful Savior)
CRUSADERS' HYMN

Anonymous German Hymn, *Munster Gesangbuch*, 1677;
translated, Source unknown, stanzas 1-3; Joseph A. Seiss, Stanza 4

Schlesische Volkslieder, 1842;
arranged by Richard S. Willis

STANDARD VERSION
Reverently (♩ = 84)

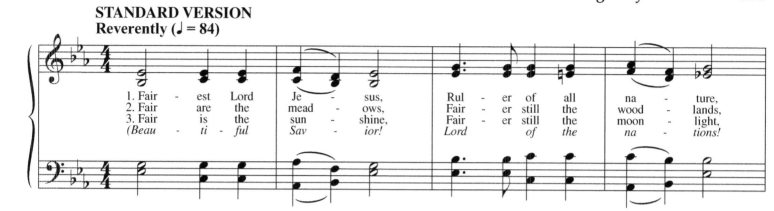

1. Fair - est Lord Je - sus,   Rul - er of all na - ture,
2. Fair are the mead - ows,   Fair - er still the wood - lands,
3. Fair is the sun - shine,   Fair - er still the moon - light,
(Beau - ti - ful Sav - ior!   Lord of the na - tions!

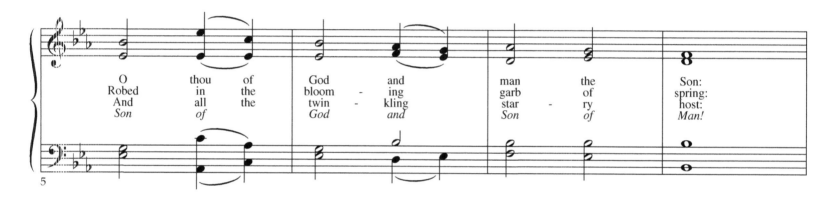

O thou of God and man the Son:
Robed in the bloom - ing garb of spring:
And all the twin - kling star - ry host:
Son of God and Son of Man!

Thee will I cher - ish, Thee will I hon - or, Thou
Je - sus is fair - er, Je - sus is pur - er, Who
Je - sus shines bright - er, Je - sus shines pur - er Than
Glo - ry and hon - or, Praise, ad - o - ra - tion, Now

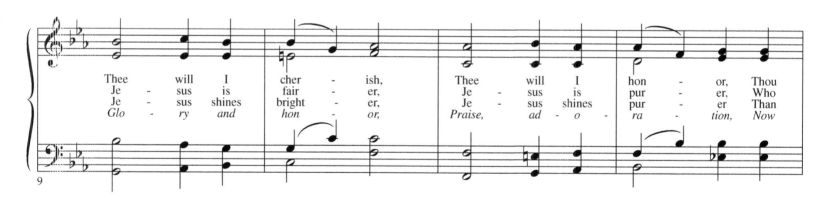

Repeat as needed (opt.) | Amen

my soul's glo - ry, joy, and crown.
makes the woe - ful heart to sing.
all the an - gels heaven can boast.
and for - ev - er more be Thine!)   A -

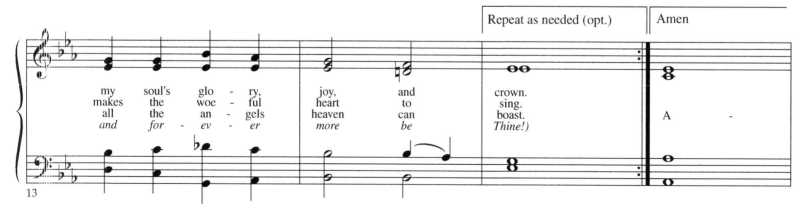

men.

VARIATION VERSE

Return to Standard Version as needed

Keyboard
(optional)

CANADIAN BRASS
FOR THE BEAUTY OF THE EARTH
DIX

Folliott S. Pierpoint, altered

Conrad Cocher;
arranged by William H. Monk

STANDARD VERSION
Joyously (♩ = 120)

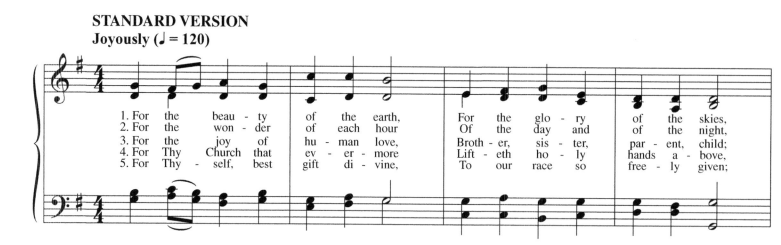

1. For the beau - ty of the earth, For the glo - ry of the skies,
2. For the won - der of each hour Of the day and of the night,
3. For the joy of hu - man love, Broth - er, sis - ter, par - ent, child;
4. For Thy Church that ev - er - more Lift - eth ho - ly hands a - bove,
5. For Thy - self, best gift di - vine, To our race so free - ly given;

For the love which from our birth O - ver and a - round us lies;
Hill and vale and tree and flower, Sun and moon and stars of light:
Friends on earth and friends a - bove; For all gen - tle thoughts and mild:
Off - ering up on ev - ery shore Her pure sac - ri - fice of love:
For that great, great love of Thine, Peace on earth and joy in heaven:

Repeat as needed (opt.)

Lord of all, to Thee we raise This our hymn of grate - ful praise.

* *rit.* is used only if the Variation Verse is played as the final verse

Return to Standard Version as needed

Keyboard
(optional)

CANADIAN BRASS

GOD OF OUR FATHERS

NATIONAL HYMN

Daniel C. Roberts

George W. Warren

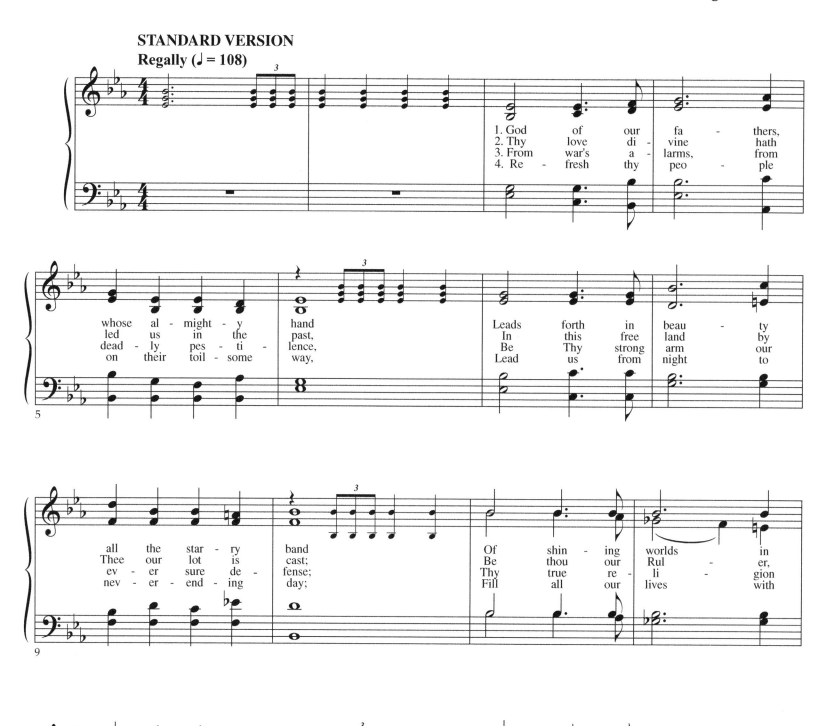

STANDARD VERSION

Regally (♩ = 108)

1. God of our fathers,
2. Thy love divine, hath
3. From war's alarms, from
4. Refresh thy people

whose almighty hand
led us in the
deadly pestilence,
on their toilsome

past,
lence,
way,

Leads forth in beauty
In this free land by
Be Thy strong arm our
Lead us from night to

all the starry
Thee our lot is
ever sure defense;
never-ending

band
cast;
day;

Of shining worlds in
Be thou our Ruler,
Thy true religion
Fill all our lives with

splendor through the
Guardian, Guide, and
in our hearts increase,
love and grace divine,

skies,
Stay,
crease,
vine,

Our grateful songs be
Thy word our law,
Thy bounteous good,
And glory, laud, and

ness and

Repeat as needed (opt.)

Amen

fore Thy throne a - rise.
paths our cho - sen way.
nour - ish us in peace.
praise be ev - er Thine!

A - men.

VARIATION VERSE

(rit.)*

* *rit.* is used only if the Variation Verse is played as the final verse

Return to Standard Version as needed

Keyboard
(optional)

CANADIAN BRASS

GUIDE ME, O THOU GREAT JEHOVAH
(God of Grace and God of Glory)

William Williams;
translated by Peter Williams

CWM RHONDDA

John Hughes

STANDARD VERSION
Earnestly (♩ = 104)

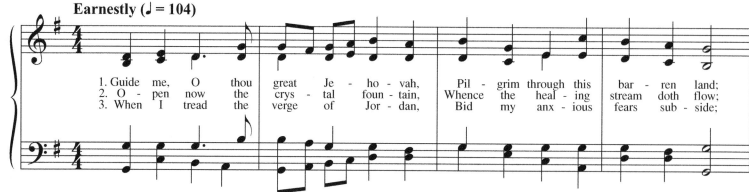

1. Guide me, O thou great Je - ho - vah, Pil - grim through this bar - ren land;
2. O - pen now the crys - tal foun - tain, Whence the heal - ing stream doth flow;
3. When I tread the verge of Jor - dan, Bid my anx - ious fears sub - side;

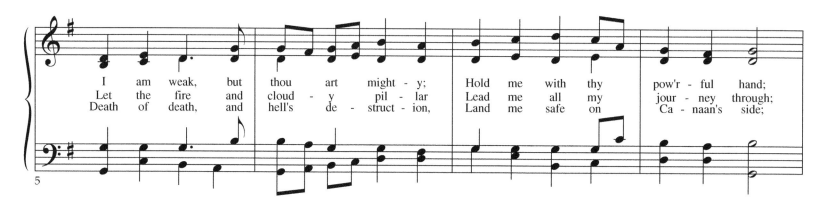

I am weak, but thou art might - y; Hold me with thy pow'r - ful hand;
Let the fire and cloud - y pil - lar Lead me all my jour - ney through;
Death of death, and hell's de - struct - ion, Land me safe on Ca - naan's side;

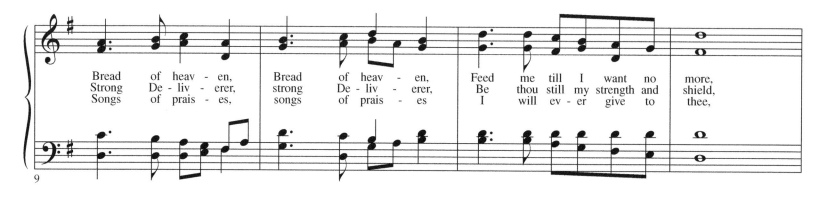

Bread of heav - en, Bread of heav - en, Feed me till I want no more,
Strong De - liv - erer, strong De - liv - erer, Be thou still my strength and shield,
Songs of prais - es, songs of prais - es I will ev - er give to thee,

Repeat as needed (opt.)

Amen

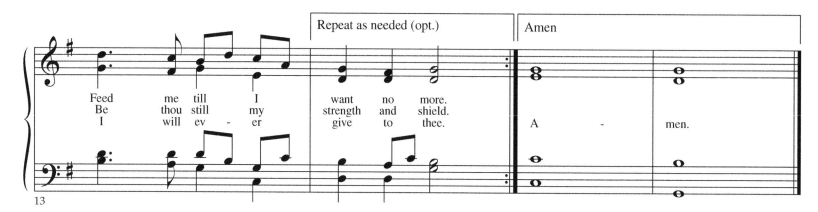

Feed me till I want no more.
Be thou still my strength and shield.
I will ev - er give to thee.

A - men.

* *rit.* is used only if the Variation Verse is played as the final verse

Return to Standard Version as needed

Keyboard
(optional)

CANADIAN BRASS

HOLY, HOLY, HOLY!

NICEA

Reginald Heber

John B. Dykes

STANDARD VERSION

Reverently (♩ = 80)

Amen

VARIATION VERSE

A - men.

(rit.)*

* *rit.* is used only if the Variation Verse is played as the final verse

Return to Standard Version as needed

Keyboard
(optional)

CANADIAN BRASS
JOYFUL, JOYFUL, WE ADORE THEE
HYMN TO JOY

Henry van Dyke

Ludwig van Beethoven

STANDARD VERSION
Joyously (♩ = 132)

* *rit.* is used only if the Variation Verse is played as the final verse

Return to Standard Version as needed

CANADIAN BRASS

LEAD ON, O KING ETERNAL

LANCASHIRE

Keyboard
(optional)

Ernest W. Shurtleff

Henry T. Smart

STANDARD VERSION

Joyously (♩ = 120)

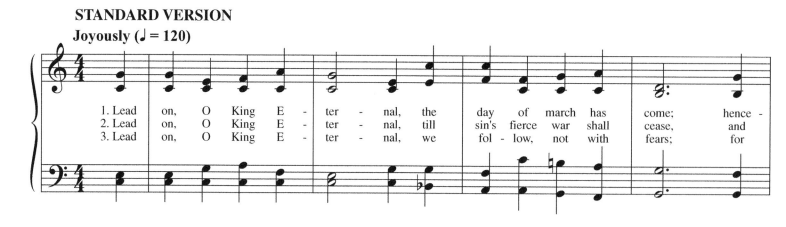

1. Lead on, O King E - ter - nal, the day of march has come; hence -
2. Lead on, O King E - ter - nal, till sin's fierce war shall cease, and
3. Lead on, O King E - ter - nal, we fol - low, not with fears; for

forth in fields of con - quest your tents shall be our home. Through days of prep - a -
ho - li - ness shall whis - per the sweet A - men of peace; for not with swords loud
glad - ness breaks like morn - ing wher - e'er your face ap - pears; for your cross is lift - ed

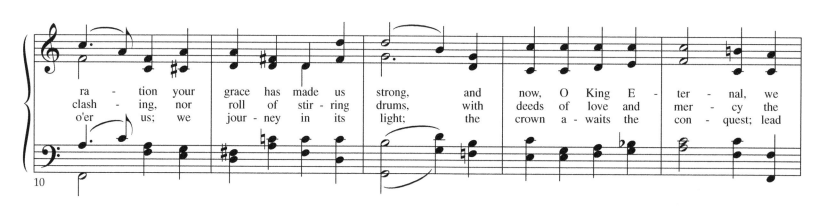

ra - tion your grace has made us strong, and now, O King E - ter - nal, we
clash - ing, nor roll of stir - ring drums, with the deeds of love and mer - cy the
o'er us; we jour - ney in its light; with the crown a - waits the con - quest; lead

Repeat as needed (opt.) | Amen

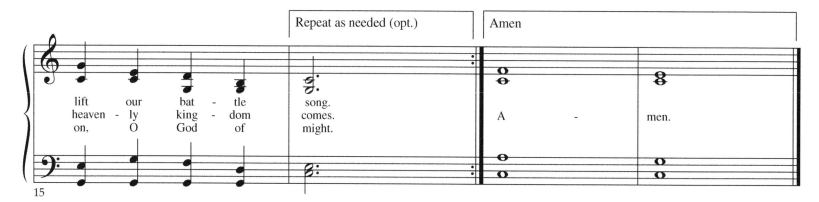

lift our bat - tle song.
heaven - ly king - dom comes. A - men.
on, O God of might.

VARIATION VERSE

* *rit.* is used only if the Variation Verse is played as the final verse

Return to Standard Version as needed

Keyboard
(optional)

CANADIAN BRASS

A MIGHTY FORTRESS IS OUR GOD

EIN FESTE BURG

Martin Luther
Trans. by F.H. Hedge, based on Psalm 46

Martin Luther

STANDARD VERSION
Steadily (♩ = 96)

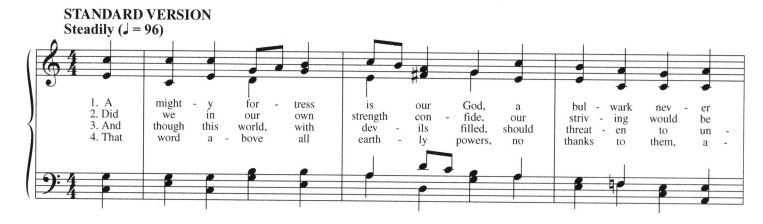

1. A might-y for-tress is our God, a bul-wark nev-er
2. Did we in our own strength con-fide, our striv-ing would be
3. And though this world, with dev-ils filled, should threat-en to un-
4. That word a-bove all earth-ly powers, no thanks to them, a-

fail - ing; our help-er he, a-mid the flood of mor-tal ills pre-
los - ing, were not the right man on our side, the man of God's own
do - us, we will not fear, for God hath willed his truth to tri - umph
bid - eth; the Spir - it and for the gifts are ours thro' him who with us

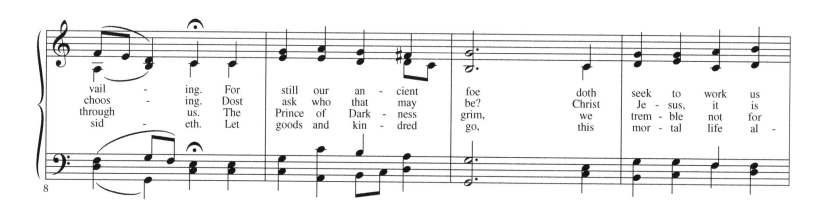

vail - ing. For still our an - cient foe doth seek to work us
choos - ing. Dost ask who that may be? Christ Je - sus, it is
through - us. The Prince of Dark - ness grim, we trem - ble not for
sid - eth. Let goods and kin - dred go, this mor - tal life al -

woe; his craft and power are great, and, armed with cru - el
he; his Lord Sa - ba - oth his name, from age to age the
him; his the rage we can en - dure, for lo, his doom is
so; the bod - y thy may kill: God's truth a - bid - eth

* *rit.* is used only if the Variation Verse is played as the final verse

Return to Standard Version as needed

Keyboard
(optional)

CANADIAN BRASS

O GOD, OUR HELP IN AGES PAST

ST. ANNE

Isaac Watts;
based on Psalm 90

attr. William Croft

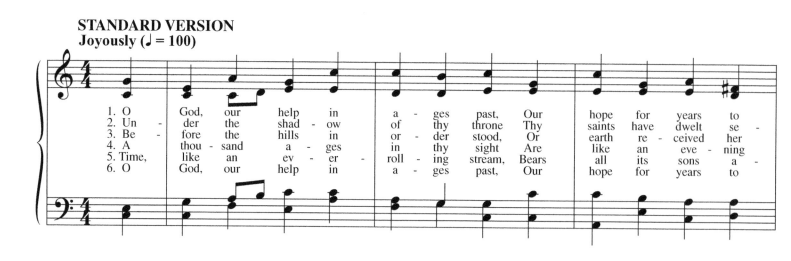

STANDARD VERSION
Joyously (♩ = 100)

1. O God, our help in a - ges past, Our hope for years to
2. Un - der the shad - ow of thy throne Thy saints have dwelt se -
3. Be - fore the hills in or - der stood, Or earth re - ceived her
4. A thou - sand a - ges in thy sight Are like an eve - ning
5. Time, like an ev - er - roll - ing stream, Bears all its sons a -
6. O God, our help in a - ges past, Our hope for years to

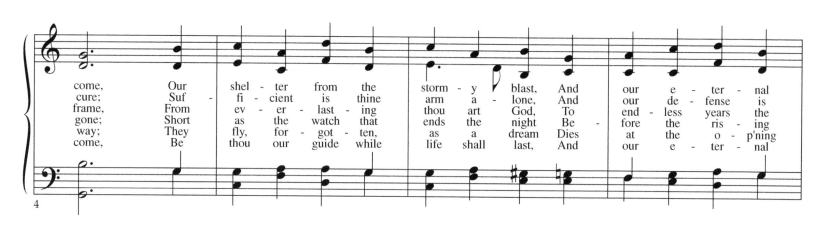

come, Our shel - ter from the storm - y blast, And our e - ter - nal
cure; Our Suf - fi - cient is thine arm a - lone, And our de - fense is
frame, From Short ev - er - last - ing thou art God, To end - less years the
gone; They as the watch that ends the night Be - fore the ris - ing
way; Be thou our guide while life shall last, And our e - ter - nal

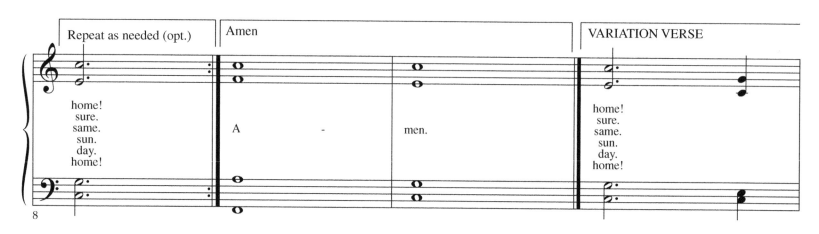

Repeat as needed (opt.)   Amen   **VARIATION VERSE**

home!   A - men.   home!
sure.   sure.
same.   same.
sun.   sun.
day.   day.
home!   home!

12

16

(rit.)*

* *rit.* is used only if the Variation Verse is played as the final verse

Return to Standard Version as needed